ZIG, ZAG AND ZOOM THROUGH THE HORSE ALPHABET

DIANE STELLHORN

S   K   P

L   I

N   C   O

A   M

Y   D   R

O   B

E   T   J

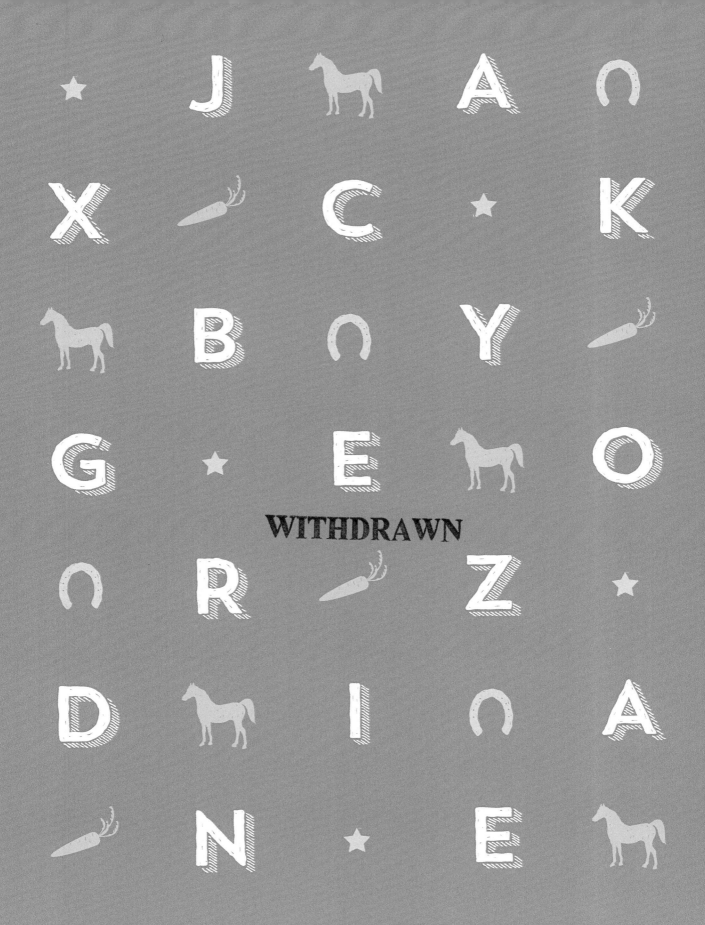

DEDICATED TO
MURREL V. LACEY

HORSEMAN EXTRAORDINAIRE,
MENTOR AND FRIEND
TO MANY HORSE LOVERS

IN LOVING MEMORY TO
BARBARA FISCHER

*a dedicated teacher and writer who inspired
and encouraged me to write this book.*

Written by Diane Stellhorn
Book Design by Big Monocle

*Copyright 2015, Big Monocle LLC
All Rights Reserved. Printed in the USA*

Acknowledgements
*I would like to thank the following
for sharing their horse expertise:
Lacey's Arabian Ranch
with Dean and Sheri Lacey,
Scott and Lorene Smith*

*Published by Big Monocle (USA) LLC., 340 S Lemon Ave, Nº 6936 Walnut, CA 91789
Library of Congress Catalog Nº 2014901490
ISBN Nº 09901471318
Juvenile/Nonfiction · Animal/Horse · Sports/Equitation · Alphabet
First Edition.*

zigzag@bigmonocle.com

ZIG, ZAG

AND

ZOOM

THROUGH THE

HORSE

ALPHABET

BY DIANE STELLHORN

**BIG
MONOCLE**

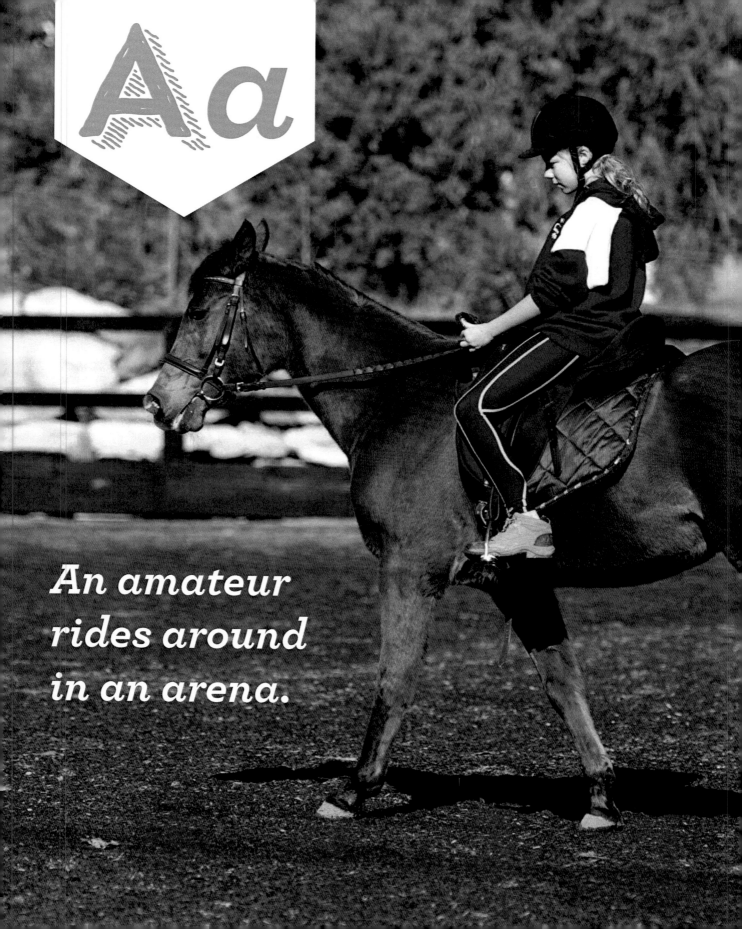

Aa

An amateur rides around in an arena.

A HORSE LOVER WHO RIDES FOR FUN IS CALLED AN AMATEUR.

Amateurs enrich their lives with the companionship of a horse, other horse lovers and family. They wish to learn more about horses by riding, joining a 4-H or horse club, reading books, watching horse shows, visiting ranches or by taking lessons from a professional horseman.

A professional horseman, for a fee, gives riding lessons. Like a coach, the pro teaches step-by-step riding skills to advance an amateur's riding levels. A pro also trains and shows amateur/owners' horses.

"PERFECT PRACTICE MAKES PERFECT."

Bb

Beautiful breeds are in the barn.

BREEDS ARE BASED ON TEMPERAMENT AND BODY TYPE.

There are over 300 breeds of horses (equine). Each purebred breed has its own registry showing a horse's bloodlines, including their sire (father) and dam (mother). Hot-blood breeds were cross-bred with cold-blood breeds developing many varieties of warm-blood breeds for a middle-weight riding and driving horse.

HOT-BLOOD BREEDS:
swift, refined, spirited

Arabian
(oldest purebred breed)

Thoroughbred
(English & Arab cross)

COLD-BLOOD BREEDS:
big, strong, workers

Draft Horses

Children cheer on colorful champions.

Horses are described by their coat color. The basic colors are bay (brown), grey (white), black and chestnut (red).

Horses of unusual and exotic coat colors are highly prized. Some have formed their own breed registries: Appaloosa, palomino, paint, pinto and buckskin.

Dd

Dream about driving a draft horse.

Bulky strong draft horses were used to carry knights in heavy armor during the Medieval Ages. In the past, they were used as a work horse: plowing farm fields and pulling logs and large wagons. Today, draft horses can be seen pulling wagons in contests and parades.

LEARN TO DRIVE UNDER THE SAFE GUIDANCE OF A PRO:

- *Harness and hitch the buggy to a trained driving horse.*
- *Use your voice and a buggy whip as aids to cue the horse's movements.*
- *Pull the reins to turn or stop.*
- *Be cautious and safe.*

Ee

Equestrians excel in English events.

An equestrian (horseback rider) enjoys showing their horsemanship at a horse show. Riders are judged on their ability to: sit balanced with good posture; control the horse at a walk, trot and canter; display showmanship.

An English equestrian may choose to perform from a variety of English styles. Each style has its own clothing attire, tack and riding form. English riders use a light, flat saddle, hold reins in both hands and post the trot.

ENGLISH STYLES INCLUDE: HUNT SEAT, JUMPING, DRESSAGE, POLO, SIDESADDLE AND SADDLE SEAT.

A foal frolics at a farm.

A mare is bred to a stallion and within 11 months she will foal (give birth). The mare will lick its foal (baby) clean and gently nudge it to stand on wobbly legs to get its first sip of milk. The mare will nurse 4 to 6 months before the foal is weaned (eats on its own).

A foal is a young horse. A yearling is one year old. A filly (female) and a colt (male) is a horse under the age of three. A stallion (male) over three may be used for breeding. A gelding (male that can no longer breed) is an ideal pleasure riding horse.

HIPPOLOGY—THE STUDY OF THE HORSE

Gg

Gently groom a grey gelding.

Grooming a horse keeps its healthy appearance, checks for sores or injuries and cleans its coat. Be safe: use a halter and tie the lead rope to a secure post; stand close to the horse; place your free hand on its body while you brush.

GROOMING INCLUDES THE CARE OF A HORSE'S HOOVES BY:

- *Safely lifting up the hoof.*

- *Picking out rocks, small debris, and manure from the frog and sole with a hoof pick.*

- *Feeling the hoof for unusual heat or pulse.*

- *Looking for signs of thrush, puncture, crack and abscess.*

- *Calling the veterinarian or farrier with any concerns.*

- *Checking for loose shoes.*

H h

Horse lovers hope to learn horsemanship.

The 4-H is a national youth club that "learns by doing". The horse project, lead by an experienced horseman, helps the 4-H member practice and learn to safely handle, care for and ride a horse. The horse group will participate in an achievement day demonstrating their skills in grooming, halter showmanship and riding.

A 4-H member may also ride in a parade, or enjoy a trail ride with their club.

JOKE

Q: WHEN DOES A HORSE WANT TO TALK?

A: "WHINNY" WANTS TO.

I i

JOKE

Q: WHY DID THE BOY STAND BEHIND THE HORSE?

A: HE THOUGHT HE MIGHT GET A KICK OUT OF IT.

It is important to be safe.

It is important to be alert and aware of your horse and its surroundings! If scared, a horse will run or strike out. Gain your horse's trust and security by your position and reaction to the horse.

ALWAYS *walk & talk calmly approaching a horse;* **NEVER** *run or yell*

ALWAYS *gently pat its neck;* **NEVER** *slap its body*

ALWAYS *clip a lead rope to the halter;* **NEVER** *grab the halter*

ALWAYS *right hand leads next to head;* **NEVER** *lead in front*

ALWAYS *left hand holds folded line;* **NEVER** *wrap line around hands or body*

ALWAYS *calmly lead at a walk;* **NEVER** *pull or jerk*

ALWAYS *go right to turn;* **NEVER** *turn left or be stepped on*

ALWAYS *wear sturdy shoes or boots;* **NEVER** *wear sandals*

ALWAYS *tie-up using a rope & halter;* **NEVER** *tie-up using reins*

"BE STRONG
ENOUGH TO
BE GENTLE."
—MURREL V. LACEY

JOKE

Q: WHAT DO POLITE HORSES DO WHEN THEY COME TO A FENCE?

A: THEY STOP AND LET YOU GO OVER FIRST.

Jj

Joyously jumping a jump.

Jumping can be extremely fun! Under the guidance of a riding instructor, learn the step-by-step jumping skills.

JUMPING SKILLS INCLUDE:

- *Using a balanced seat with hand and leg aids at all gaits from walk to gallop.*

- *Trotting over caveletti poles with even strides.*

- *Using leg and seat aids to encourage the horse to jump over rails.*

- *Looking forward beyond the jump.*

- *Lifting slightly up, heels down and lean forward as the horse lifts its forequarters over the rail.*

- *Jumping with hands on the horse's neck while giving with the reins.*

- *Landing gently in the saddle and bringing the hands back to normal position.*

- *Advancing to more difficult jumps with lots of practice.*

15

Kk

Kudos to the Kentucky Derby winner.

The Kentucky Derby is a mile and quarter race for the fastest three year old thoroughbred horses. The winner of the race goes home with a rose garland, a prized trophy and over a million dollars. It is the most exciting two minutes in sports!

"SECRETARIAT" HOLDS THE RECORD OF THE FASTEST KENTUCKY DERBY WINNER AT 1:59.40. HE WAS ALSO A TRIPLE CROWN WINNER.

There are many thoroughbred farms in America hoping to breed and raise a winning race horse. The farm owner will breed his mare to a proven fast stallion. The foal will be raised running free in lush pastures, given the best health care and carefully trained for the racetrack.

Lunging a leaping Lipizzaner.

A lunging horse moves in a circle around the handler while connected to a lunge line (rope). The handler uses his voice, position with the horse and a lunge whip to teach the horse control and its gaits. Before riding, lunging helps to warm-up your horse.

A HANDLER LUNGES A HORSE BY:

- *Clipping a 30 foot lunge line to a halter or cavesson.*

- *Holding the line in the hand closest to the head and the whip in the hand closest to the tail (as in a triangle).*

- *Cueing the horse to move forward, away from the handler, by "clucking", saying "walk" and/or "snapping" the lunge whip (adds pressure).*

- *Moving in a small circle facing the shoulder, slowly releasing line to enlarge the circle. Be ready to react to the horse's position.*

- *Changing gaits by stepping sideways toward the hip (adds movement) or head (slows movement) and saying "trot, canter/lope or whoa".*

Mustangs meander in a meadow.

A mustang is a hardy wild (free roaming) horse. Over 100 years ago, about two million mustangs roamed the desert, valleys, hills and mountains of North America. These horses originally escaped from Spanish explorers. Later, freed horses from pioneers, soldiers, ranchers and owners joined the wild herds.

TODAY THERE ARE ABOUT 25,000 WILD MUSTANGS.

Most wild mustangs live freely in protected reserves in Nevada, Oregon, Montana and Wyoming. The Wild Free-roaming Horse and Burro Act was created for mustang management and to allow interested horsemen to adopt. You will need lots of patience and knowledge of horse training to change a wild mustang into a pleasure horse.

Mm

Nn

Nutritious feed is nipped and nibbled.

JOKE

Q: WHY DID THE HORSE CROSS THE ROAD?

A: BECAUSE SOMEBODY SHOUTED HAY!

Horses are grazing animals, meant to slowly eat and digest pasture grass or hay all day long. The amount of feed varies with a horse's size, age, health and work.

FEEDING RULES INCLUDE:

- *Checking your horse's condition daily.*

- *Providing small amounts of feed often at the same time each day.*

- *Making no sudden changes in the diet.*

- *Keeping the feed and feed area clean.*

- *Graining active and work horses in specified amounts.*

- *Never working a stalled horse immediately after eating.*

- *Providing mineral blocks, vitamins and always fresh water.*

Observing outstanding equestrians at the Olympics.

Every four years, the best horse/rider teams come from many countries to compete in the Summer Olympics. It is the highest honor to win a gold, silver or bronze medal for your country.

THE OLYMPIC EVENTS INCLUDE:

- *Dressage - equestrians performing the highest level of required classical movements.*

- *Show jumping - jumping over high and wide obstacles. The horse/rider with the fewest penalties and fastest time wins.*

- *Three day eventing - testing skills, speed and endurance. The first day is a dressage test. The second day is a cross country course covering about five miles of galloping over obstacles: log piles, walls, brush fences, ditches and banks. The last day is a shorter jump and steeplechase course.*

A proud pony prances in a parade.

A pony is a small horse under the height of 14.2 hands (58 inches) measured from the ground to the withers. Ponies are strong and hardy, characterized by: sturdy bones; thick coat, tail and mane; short legs; thick necks with short, wide heads. There are many breeds of ponies.

A PONY, WITH TRAINING, CAN BE USED FOR:

• Children to ride.

• Parade or show.

• Driving.

• Working by pulling or carrying loads.

JOKE

Q: WHAT DID THE PONY SAY WHEN HE HAD A SORE THROAT?

A: I AM A LITTLE HOARSE.

Qq

Quarter horses are quick and quiet.

The American Quarter Horse is the most popular breed in the USA. Its name came from winning races of a quarter mile against other breeds. Some have been clocked at 55 mph. A quarter horse's power comes from its muscular body, strong hindquarters and broad chest.

The quarter horse performs in many western events such as: reining (using its "cow sense" to move cattle), roping, barrel racing and ranch work. It is an ideal show horse, all-round pleasure and family horse due to its quiet, gentle and willing personality.

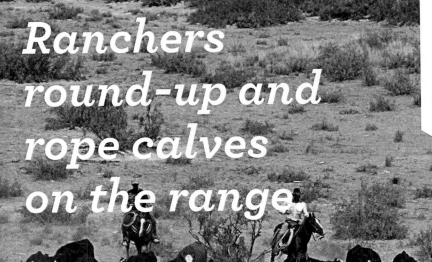

Ranchers round-up and rope calves on the range.

R r

Ranchers hold annual spring round-ups to gather cattle from spread-out grazing lands into holding corrals.

COWBOYS AND GIRLS WILL USE A STURDY STOCK HORSE TO HELP DO THEIR WORK INCLUDING:

- *Cutting (separating) calves from the herd.*

- *Roping, throwing and tying the calf's three legs together.*

- *Identifying a calf by tagging an ear and branding a hip.*

- *Vaccinating against diseases.*

- *Checking for any health needs.*

- *Herding cattle up a chute into a cattle trailer to be moved to new grazing land.*

Ss

Saddle-up, sit-up & smile as you ride your steed.

Mount a horse in an open area.

SIT CORRECTLY IN THE SADDLE BY:

- *Sitting relaxed with straight posture (shoulders, hips and heels in line).*

- *Keeping contact with the horse's body by using the legs' inside thigh and upper calf.*

- *Placing weight on the balls of the feet in the stirrups (heels down and ankles flexible).*

- *Holding the reins in one hand just above and in front of the horn (curb bit), or in both hands at the sides of the horn or pommel (snaffle bit).*

- *Keeping arms and hands relaxed with elbows close to the sides of the body (all in line with the bit).*

- *Now smile, move with the horse and enjoy the ride!*

Tend to your trusty tack.

Tack is necessary equipment to work a horse. Ask the advice of a knowledgable horseman as to the type of tack best suited for you and your horse (the simpler, the better). Be sure all tack fits correctly. There is specific tack for training, trail riding, English, western, driving and many more uses.

TACK NEEDS CONSTANT CARE BY:

- Using a damp cloth and glycerine soap to remove dirt.

- Oiling any leather to keep its moisture.

- Making a safety check for any wear, tear or weakness.

- Storing tack in a tack room or dry tack box.

"HOME IS WHERE YOUR HEART IS, SO I'LL BE IN THE BARN!"

Uu

Utilize your useful aids.

An equestrian uses aids to cue and guide a horse's movements. An experienced rider's slightest cue will get a response from a well-trained horse. The rider uses pressure and release. The natural aids include the rider's balanced seat, quiet legs, soft hands and voice. Artificial aids (objects a rider wears or carries to add pressure or discipline to a horse) includes bits, spurs, crops and whips.

EQUESTRIANS COMMUNICATE TO A HORSE BY USING:

- Legs - to move the horse forward, backward, sideways, add power and/or stop.

- Hands - to confine the horse's power, ask it to go in a certain direction and/or stop (from reins to bit).

- Seat - to cue the horse's movement, gaits and direction by moving with the horse's hips and shoulders and shifting the weight of your seat.

Veterinarians give vaccinations.

A veterinarian is an animal doctor. A horse vet gives vaccinations, diagnoses, treats sick horses, cares for injuries and performs surgery. A vet gives advice to horsemen about the proper care for a healthy active horse.

A HORSE OWNER'S RESPONSIBILITIES INCLUDE:

- *Observing any changes in the horse's health: behavior or mood; eating or drinking; nasal discharge or coughing; temperature or pulse rate; manure; movement (lameness).*

- *Keeping the veterinarian and farriers' phone numbers posted, writing symptoms and vet's instructions.*

- *Keeping a horse first-aid kit.*

- *Owning a veterinarian handbook.*

29

Ww

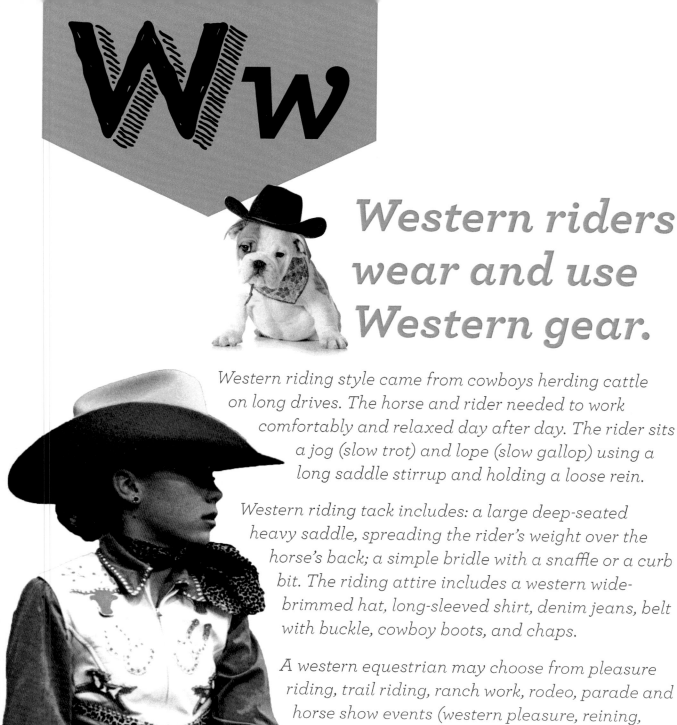

Western riders wear and use Western gear.

Western riding style came from cowboys herding cattle on long drives. The horse and rider needed to work comfortably and relaxed day after day. The rider sits a jog (slow trot) and lope (slow gallop) using a long saddle stirrup and holding a loose rein.

Western riding tack includes: a large deep-seated heavy saddle, spreading the rider's weight over the horse's back; a simple bridle with a snaffle or a curb bit. The riding attire includes a western wide-brimmed hat, long-sleeved shirt, denim jeans, belt with buckle, cowboy boots, and chaps.

A western equestrian may choose from pleasure riding, trail riding, ranch work, rodeo, parade and horse show events (western pleasure, reining, cutting, stock horse, working cow horse, roping and trail).

"X" marks the campsite after an extra exciting trail ride!

Trail riding and horse camping is an exciting adventure sharing new terrain (streams, logs, forests, steep narrow trails, ocean beaches and many surprises from nature) with your horse, family and friends.

RIDE TRAILS SAFELY BY:

- *Trusting and being secure with your horse; watching your horse's body language and being ready to react.*

- *Riding with experienced horsemen on a marked trail.*

- *Using a conditioned, well-trained calm horse.*

- *Pre-checking the horse's health, hooves and tack.*

- *Packing a saddle bag including: a first-aid kit; food; water; rubber easyboot; hoof-pick and pocket knife; flashlight; halter and lead rope.*

- *Following the "trail boss" single-file, with at least one horse distance between riders. Be courteous.*

- *Walking up and down steep hills.*

- *Walking the first and last mile.*

- *Encouraging the horse to go through difficult terrain by keeping its attention. "A horse may be stumped by a stump."*

Young equestrians yell out "yahoo"!

OTHER HORSE ACTIVITIES TO TRY:

- Parades

- Vaulting

- Competitive endurance rides

- Competitive trail rides

- Polo

- Mounted police, park ranger and rescue unit

- Ride-and-tie (one horse and two people taking turns running and riding)

- Organized riding games (dollar bill marathon, egg and spoon race, key-hole race, pass the baton)

- Drill team

- Gymkhana

- Therapeutic riding

- Horse packing/camping

- Field (fox) hunter

"RIDING: THE ART OF KEEPING THE HORSE BETWEEN YOU AND THE GROUND."

Zz

Zig, zag and zoom with zest!

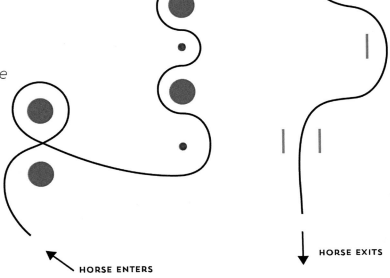

HORSE ENTERS

HORSE EXITS

Gymkhana is a patterned obstacle race that shows the skill, speed and handiness of a horse/rider team. The events include: barrel racing, keyhole race, keg race, flag race and pole bending. Watch or participate at: rodeos, and/or state, regional and local club competitions or play days.

TIPS FOR GYMKHANA RIDERS INCLUDE:

- Maintaining focus and a balanced seat.

- Coordinating hand and leg aids for lead, bend and gait.

- Learning the pattern, from slow to faster.

- Wearing the correct attire: western shirt, pants, belt, cowboy boots and cowboy hat/helmet.

- Practicing with a gymkhana group and/or pro.

JOKE

Q: WHAT DID THE HORSE SAY WHEN HE FELL?

A: "I'VE FALLEN AND I CAN'T GIDDY-UP."

DIAGRAMS

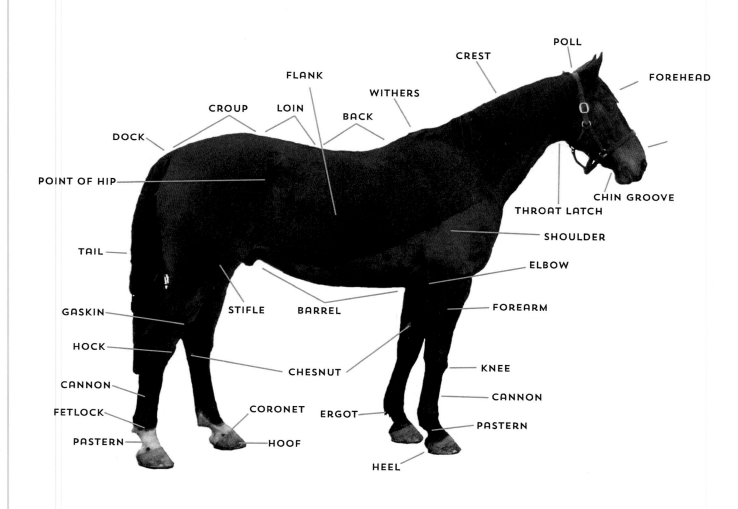

CREST
POLL
FLANK
FOREHEAD
WITHERS
CROUP   LOIN
BACK
DOCK
POINT OF HIP
CHIN GROOVE
THROAT LATCH
SHOULDER
TAIL
ELBOW
GASKIN
FOREARM
STIFLE   BARREL
HOCK
CHESNUT
KNEE
CANNON
CANNON
FETLOCK
CORONET   ERGOT
PASTERN
PASTERN
HOOF
HEEL

EMERGENCY CHARTS

VITAL SIGNS

ADULT HORSE:

Temperature: 99.5-101.5 F

Heart Rate: 32-44 beats/min

Respiratory Rate: 6-16 breaths/min

Mucous Membrane Color: Pale Pink

Capillary Refill Time: 1-2 seconds

Gut Sounds: Always Present

FOALS:

Temperature: increases the 1st 4 days that plateaus at 100-102 F

Heart Rate: 60-110 beats/min

Respiratory Rate: 25-60 breaths/min

FIRST AID KIT

- *Stethoscope*
- *Thermometer*
- *Scissors*
- *Hemostat*
- *4x4 gauze*
- *6" gauze roll*
- *Vet wrap*
- *Elastikon tape*
- *Ophthalmic Oint.*
- *Telfa pads*
- *Light*
- *Duct tape*
- *Salt*
- *Plastic bowl*
- *Water-soluble antibacterial ointment*
- *Antiseptic soap (Betadine Scrub)*
- *Antiseptic solution (Betadine)*
- *Sheet or Roll cotton*
- *Medication (if possible)*
- *SMZ-TMS*
- *Phenylbutazone or Banamine*

BASIC FIRST AID

LACERATIONS:

- *Control hemorrhage with bandaid of direct pressure*
- *Clean contaminated wounds with clear water, antiseptic soap*
- *Control swelling with bandage*
- *Attention to punctures*

COLIC:

- *Mild to moderate pain-obtain vital signs then call for assistance/advice*
- *No food - walk 10-15 min, rest 30 min*
- *Severe or unrelenting pain - call veterinarian now!*

LAMENESS:

- *Look for heat and swelling*
- *Apply cold 20-30 min*
- *Minimize swelling, support and immobilize with a bandage.*
- *Nothing apparent - it's in the foot until proven otherwise.*

EYE PROBLEM:

- *Clean/flush with salt solution or water*
- *Cold compress if swollen*
- *Antibiotic ophthalmic ointment*
- *Call veterinary clinic for assistance/advice.*

PARTURITION:

- *Stage II (breaking water)- 10-30 min and making progress, "diving" position with staggered front legs then head, if mal-positioned or no progress --call for assistance.*
- *Stage III (pass afterbirth)- Should pass placenta within 4 hours, examine for entirety.*
- *Wash mare around vulva and udder to dilute contamination*
- *Foal should stand and nurse within 2 hours, dip navel with aniseptic solution.*

WESTERN SADDLE

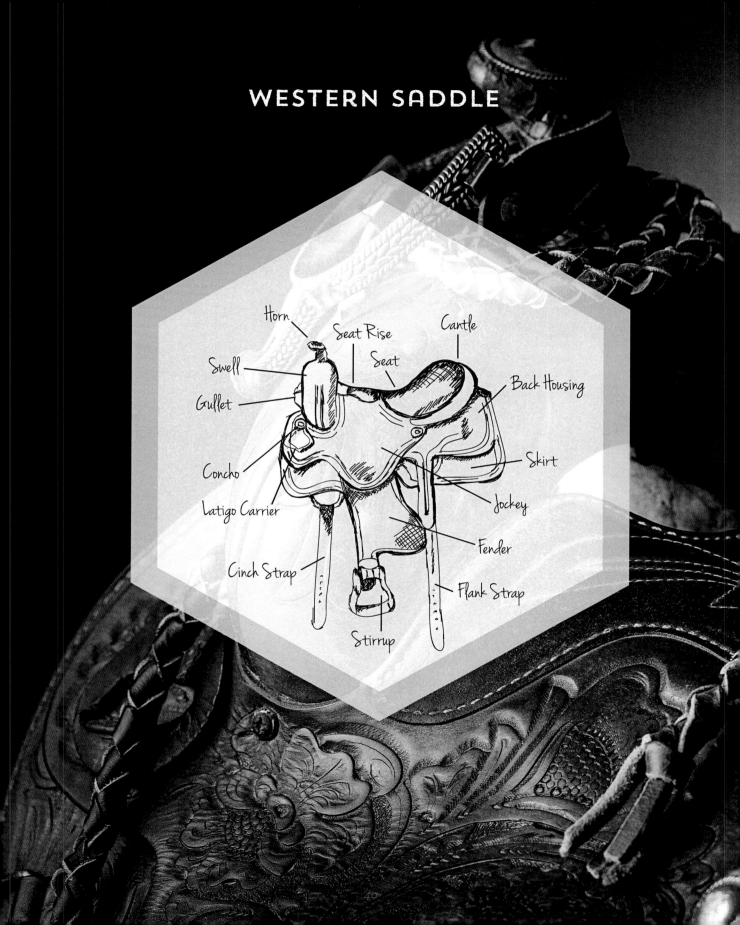

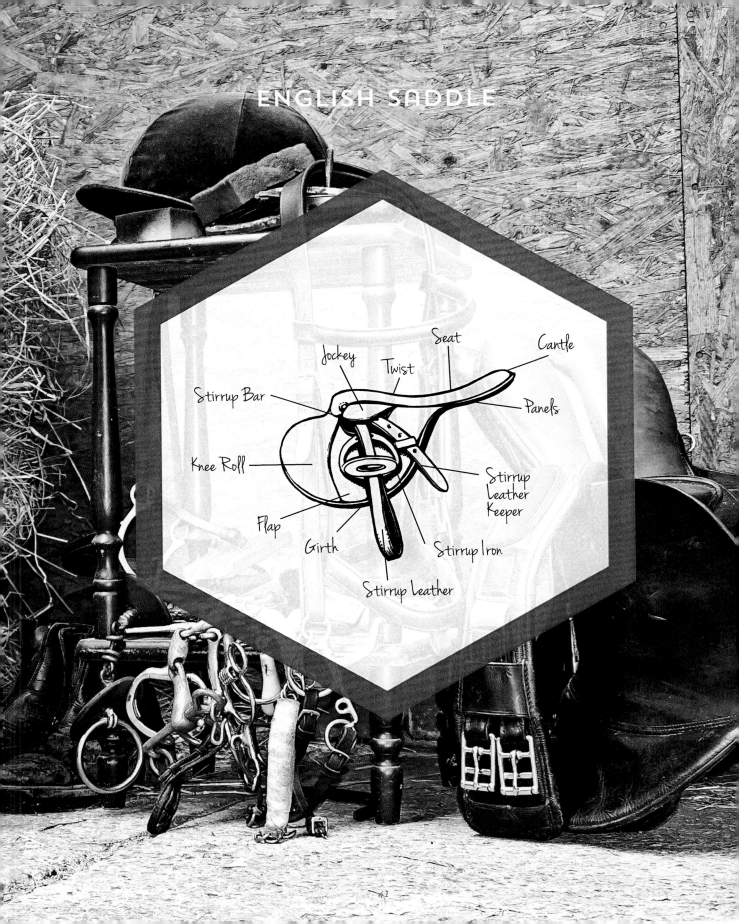

Jockey

Twist

Seat

Cantle

Stirrup Bar

Panels

Knee Roll

Stirrup Leather Keeper

Flap

Girth

Stirrup Iron

Stirrup Leather

BRIDLE

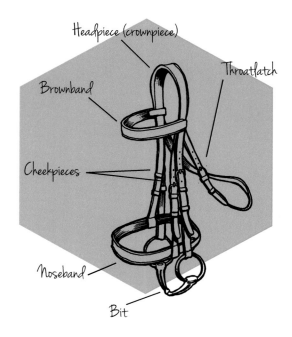

Headpiece (crownpiece)

Throatlatch

Brownband

Cheekpieces

Noseband

Bit

HALTER

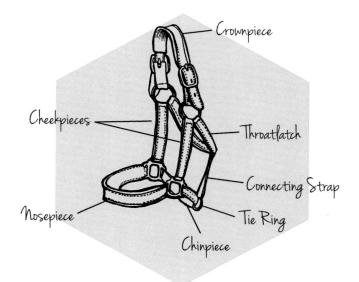

Crownpiece

Cheekpieces

Throatlatch

Connecting Strap

Tie Ring

Nosepiece

Chinpiece

INDEX

Amateur 3

Anatomy 38

Appaloosa 6

Arabian 3

Breeds 5

Coat 6

Cold-blooded 5

Color 6

Cowboy 25, 30

Dam 5

Draft horse 3, 5, 7

Dressage 8, 22

Driving 7

English 8, 41

Equestrian 8, 22, 28, 35

Equestrian sports 15, 22, 35, 37

Eventing 22

Farrier 10

Feeding 21, 29

Filly 9

First aid 29, 39

Foal 9

Gelding 10

Grazing 21

Grooming 10

Gymkhana 35, 37

Hoof 10

Horsemanship 8

Hot-blood 5

Hunt 8

Jumping 15, 22

Kentucky Derby 17

Lungeing 18

Mare 9

Mount 26

Nutrition 21

Paint 6

Mustang 19

Olympics 22

Polo 8, 35

Palomino 6

Pinto 6

Pony 23

Post 8

Professional 3, 7

Quarter horse 24

Racing 17, 24, 35, 37

Ranchers 5

Registry 5, 6

Riding aids 28

Saddle 8, 26, 40, 41

Saftey 12

Sidesaddle 8

Sire 5

Stallion 9

Tack 27, 40, 41

Thoroughbred 3, 17

Trail Riding 33

Veterinarian 10, 29, 39

Warm-blood 5

Western 24, 30

GLOSSARY

AIDS - *signals from the rider or driver to tell the horse what the handler wants it to do*

AMATEUR - *one who rides as a pastime not as a professional*

APPALOOSA - *a spotted breed originating from the Nez Perce Indians*

ARABIAN - *oldest breed originating from the Arabian desert, noted for small size, dished face, erect carriage, high intelligence, and lively disposition*

ARENA - *an enclosed area with a fence and gate used for riding and training horses*

BARREL RACING - *a sport in which a horse/rider races around barrels*

BIT - *a metal mouthpiece connected to a bridle and reins*

BREEDS - *a group of horses with distinct genetics, animals for each breed are kept in official stud books*

BRIDLE - *the entire headpiece, headstall, chin strap, throat-latch, bit and reins used to control a horse*

BUCKSKIN - *a golden tan colored horse*

CANTER - *a gait between walk and gallop with three beats*

CAVALETTI - *wooden posts placed on or close to the ground, a certain measured distance, over which you ride your horse*

CHAPS - *leather leggings worn over pants and buckled around the waist*

COLIC - *a horse with intestinal pain, ranging from mild to life-threatening severe (number one cause of death)*

COMPETITIVE TRAIL RIDING - *a sport in which english or western riders negotiate a preset trail, and are judged on horsemanship and fitness of their mount, instead of speed*

CONFORMATION - *the physical structure and appearance*

CURB BIT - *a bit that uses a side piece (shank) and a strap or chain under the chin for leverage on the bars of the mouth*

CUTTING - *a judged event in which a horse/rider pair must separate one calf from the herd and keep it from returning to the herd*

DRESSAGE - *an event in which the horse/rider performs individually to show mastery of required movements, involving the gradual training of the horse in stages*

DRILL TEAM - *a riding group performing choreographed maneuvers to music*

ENDURANCE RIDING - *an event in which horse/rider compete over a long distance trail to test their physical condition, respiratory recovery rate and stamina*

EQUESTRIAN - *a person who rides horses*

EQUINE - *a horse or another member of the horse family*

FARRIER - *a craftsman that trims and shoes a horse's hooves*

FROG - *the dense, shock-absorbing, triangular growth at the underside of the hoof*

GAITS - *the different ways a horse travels, from walk, trot, jog, canter or lope, and gallop*

GALLOP - *the fastest pace of a horse, with all the hooves off the ground at the same time*

GELDING - *a castrated male horse*

LAME - *a term used to describe a horse limping or showing signs of leg or foot problems*

LOPE - *a slow canter performed by western horses*

MOUNT - *to get up on a horse*

PALOMINO - *a horse of gold color with a white mane and tail*

PAINT or **PINTO** - *horse with a two-toned coat*

POLO - *a team sport played on horseback using a mallet to hit a ball.*

POSTING -*rising and sitting in the saddle at the trot, in rhythm with the horse's strides, taking the "bounce" out of the trot*

PROFESSIONAL - *a horseman that is paid for his horse expertise*

REINING - *an event in which a western horse/rider pair perform a pattern of circles and straight lines, with spinning turns and slidding stops*

REINS - *the leather lines attached to the bit and held in the rider's hands to control and guide a horse*

ROPING - *a timed event in which a western rider chases and ropes a steer*

SADDLE SEAT - *a form of English riding of gaited horses of high flashy action*

SIDESADDLE - *riding a type of saddle that allows you to ride aside*

SNAFFLE BIT - *a bit with a joined mouth-piece and rings at the ends; works on the corners of the mouth*

STEED - *a lively spirited horse*

STIRRUPS - *the part of the saddle that supports your feet*

STOCK HORSE - *a horse used to herd and manage livestock on a ranch*

SURCINGLE - *webbing strap that surrounds a horse's barrel*

TACK - *the gear used on a horse (bridle, saddle)*

THOROUGHBRED - *an English breed tracing to three Arabian sires. The world's premier race horse, also used in jumping.*

THRUSH - *a foul-smelling infectious condition of the frog of the hoof, usually from standing in wet soiled bedding*

TROT - *a two-beat gait between walk and canter*

VAULTING - *gymnastic maneuvers performed on the back of a lunged cantering horse wearing a bridle with side-reins attached to a surcingle with two grab rings.*

VETERINARIAN - *Doctor of Veterinarian Medicine (DMV) is a person trained to provide medical care of animals*

WALK - *a four-beat gait, slowest of all the natural gaits of a horse.*

WEANLING - *a foal weaned from its mother, but less than a year old.*

WITHERS - *the bony part at the base of the neck*

HOW FAST IS YOUR HORSE GOING?

WALK

3-4 mph

TROT

8-10 mph

GALLOP

26-30 mph

IMAGE CREDITS

P. 3 - *Photo by: Daniel Pertovt*
*http://www.flickr.com/photos/16269376@
N00/5798838800/*

P.3 - *Photo by: Jeff Bean*

P. 3 - *Photo by: Jeffrey Little*

P. 4 - *Photo by: Dennis Jarvis*
*http://www.flickr.com/photos/22490717@
N02/3848016746/*

P. 5-*Photo by: Carine06*
*http://www.flickr.com/photos/43555660@
N00/9728145468/*

P. 5-*Photo by: Roger H. Goun*
*http://www.flickr.com/photos/
sskennel/2480920429/in/photostream/*

P. 5 - *Photo by: Trescastillos*
*http://en.wikipedia.org/wiki/
File:LaMirage_body07.jpg#file*

P. 5 - *Photo by: Richard*
*http://commons.wikimedia.org/wiki/
File:Belgian_draft_horse2.jpg*

P. 5 - *Photo by: Starley Shelton*
*http://www.flickr.com/photos/52349296@
N08/6329221530/*

P. 6 - *Photo by: purpleswimmergirl2*
*http://purpleswimmergirl2.deviantart.
com/art/Free-Use-Pre-Cut-Horse-
Stock-1-308005972*

P. 6 - *Photo by: Bill Vidigal*
*http://upload.wikimedia.org/wikipedia/
commons/f/f7/Mangalarga_Marchador_
Conform%C3%A7%C3%A30.jpeg*

P. 6 - *Photo by: Peripitus*
*http://commons.wikimedia.org/wiki/
File:Palamino_horse.JPG*

P. 6 - *Photo by: Carole Ducos*
*http://commons.wikimedia.org/wiki/
File:Avenger_-_Westphalian_horse.jpg*

P. 6 - *Photo by: David Lewis*
*http://www.flickr.com/photos/28930798@
N04/8042067947/*

P. 6 - *Photo by: Darrell Dodds*
*http://en.wikipedia.org/wiki/
File:THIEL_619.jpg*

P. 7 - *Photo by: Paul Keleher*
*http://www.flickr.com/photos/57253263@
N00/2339355350/*

P. 17 - *Photo by: Craig Duncan*
https://en.wikipedia.org/wiki/File:KY_Derby_ROSES_1.jpeg

P. 17 - *Photo by: Quang Ho*
Shutterstock pic #127513112

P. 18 - *Photo by: Axel Bührmann*
http://www.flickr.com/photos/9852972@N03/3066355546

P. 19 - *Photo by: dbarronoss*
http://www.flickr.com/photos/56398280@N00/325530648/

P. 20 - *Photo by: Don J Schulte*
http://www.flickr.com/photos/29392873@N07/6520566139/

P. 21 - *Photo by: Anna Hoychuk*
Shutterstock pic # 53849239

P. 21 - *Photo by: Jiang Hongyan*
Shutterstock pic # 144379045

P. 22 - *Photo by: Manik*
http://www.flickr.com/photos/23703495@N07/2626736642/

P. 22 - *Photo by: smudge9000*
http://www.flickr.com/photos/7599112@N08/9453055700/

P. 22 - *Photo by: Ping Timeout*
http://www.flickr.com/photos/10757800@N00/4910400540/

P. 22 - *Photo by: Henry Bucklow*
https://en.wikipedia.org/wiki/File:Badminton_horse_trials_open_ditch_jump.jpg

P. 23 - *Photo by: Matt Gillman*
http://www.flickr.com/photos/37865761@N03/3654794618/

P. 23 - *Photo by: Emmanuel Keller*
http://www.flickr.com/photos/8070463@N03/3629207036/

P. 23 - *Photo by: Emmanuel Keller*
http://www.flickr.com/photos/8070463@N03/3629259105/

P. 23 - *Photo by: popofatticus*
https://secure.flickr.com/photos/49503214348@N01/2189603107

P. 24 - *Photo by: Al_HikesAZ*
http://www.flickr.com/photos/7202153@N03/3354741725/

P. 24 - - *Photo by: Michael Zupon*
http://www.flickr.com/photos/30872191@N00/3629085448/

P. 24 - *Photo by: billypoonphotos*
https://upload.wikimedia.org/wikipedia/commons/1/13/Photo_Quarter_Horse_Racing.jpg

P. 25 - *Photo by: Brian Schack*
http://en.wikipedia.org/wiki/File:Cattle_round_up.jpg

REFERENCES

MORE INFORMATION AVAILABLE AT THE FOLLOWING SOURCES:

A: cha-ahse.org (certified horsemanship association)

B: wikipedia.org/wiki/list-of-horse-breeds, arabianhorses.org/education

   4-h.org/resource-library/curriculum/4-h-horse/giddy-up-and-go

C: wikipedia.org/wiki/equine-coat-color

   4-h.org/resource-library/curriculum/4-h-horse/giddy-up-and-go

D: wikipedia.org/wiki/draft_horse, Youtube.com/watch?v=?vGYvH6t_CZA

E: wikipedia.org/wiki/English_riding

   youtube.com/watch?feature=related&v=WPqpfeklaK4

F: 4-h.org/resource-library/curriculum/4-h-horse/stable-management

G: 4-h.org/resource-library/curriculum/4-h-horse/head-heart-hooves

H: 4-h.org/resource-library/curriculum/4-h-horse

I: allridersup.com/PDF/basic horse safety,

   4-h.org/resource-library/curriculum/4-h-horse/giddy-up

J: http://en.wikipedia.org/wiki/Jumping_(horse)

K: kentuckyderby.com/horse, horsebreedslist.com/horse-breeds/101/thoroughbred

L: 4-h.org/resource-library/curriculum/4-h-horse/riding-the-range

M: wildhorseandburro.blm.org

N: wikipedia.org/wiki/equine_nutrition4-h.org/resource-library/curriculum/4-h

O: olympicequestrian.com

P: wikipedia.org/wiki/pony, pony-club.org

Q: wikipedia.org/wiki/quarterhorse, aqha.org

R: yoûtube.com/watch?v=tid-WmMXUQ, youtube/AQHA

   Wikipedia.org/wiki/cowboy

S: *YouTube.com/watch?v=6NLWL2WJx-A*

4-h.org/resource-library/curriculum/4-h-horse/

T: *YouTube.com/watch?v=6NLWL2WJx-A*

4-h.org/resource-library/curriculum/4-h-horse/

U: *wikipedia.org/wiki/riding_aids, 4-h.org/resource-library/curriculum/4-h-horse*

V: *petmed.com/horse, 4-h.org/resource-library/curriculum/4-h-horse/riding-the-range*

4-h.org/resource-library/curriculum/4-h-horse/stable-management

W: *equiworld.net/uk/sports/western_riding*

4-h.org/resource-library/curriculum/4-h-horse/riding-the-range

X: *teviscup.org, horseandmuletrails.com,*

4-h.org/research-library/curriculum/4-h-horse/riding-the-range

Y: *voices.yahoo.com/horsebackriding_games_activities, equisearch.com/horses_riding training/paradeswikipedia.org/wiki/list_equestrian_sports, americanvaulting.org, youtube.com/watch?v=b2XI?RjsvUNU*

wikipedia.org/wiki/equestrian_drill_team

Z: *wikipedia.org/wiki/gymkhana_(equestrian)*

calgymkhana.com/about/about_training

MORE: *wikipedia.org,4-h.org/resource-library/curriculum/4-h-horse, laceysarabians.com , ucdavisvtms.org, aqha.org , olympicequestrian.org.*

The information in this book is meant to supplement, not replace, proper equitation training, correct equipment and safety knowledge.

L U V

H O

R S E

A R

B I N

D O

G Y Z

F O

B Z K

M S

W Q J

C H

R I S

T X

Made in the USA
San Bernardino, CA
02 October 2015